LIFE IN THE SLOTH LANE

LIFE IN THE SLOTH LANE

LUCY COOKE

WORKMAN PUBLISHING • NEW YORK

All the sloths featured in this book were rescued as babies by sanctuaries in Central America. In most cases, their mothers had been stolen for the pet or tourism trade or killed by power lines, dogs, or roads. All these orphans were part of rehabilitation programs to return them to the wild as adults, where they belong.

In the wild, sloths like to occupy a surprisingly large home range and are solitary in nature. They may look like they are smiling all the time, but they do not like to be kept in small enclosures or handled by humans. If you love sloths, please respect their nature: Never try to pet or hold one (for a selfie or a hug) and support organizations—like those listed on page 140—that do not keep sloths captive in inappropriate conditions.

Copyright © 2018 by Lucy Cooke

Photos copyright © by Lucy Cooke

Library of Congress Cataloging-in-Publication Data is available.

ISBN 978-0-7611-9322-7

Design by Stephen Hughes

Workman books are available at special discounts when purchased in bulk for premiums and sales promotions as well as for fund-raising or educational use. Special editions or book excerpts can also be created to specification. For details, contact the Special Sales Director at the address below, or send an email to specialmarkets@workman.com.

Workman Publishing Co., Inc.
225 Varick Street
New York, NY 10014-4381
workman.com

WORKMAN is a registered trademark of Workman Publishing Co., Inc.

Printed in China

First printing March 2018

10 9 8 7 6 5 4 3 2 1

INTRODUCTION

Sloths are the perfect role models for a more mindful existence. I believe their laid-back lifestyle has much to teach the human race, and that's why I founded the Sloth Appreciation Society after years of documenting and observing these amazing creatures. We humans—busy bipedal apes who are determined to move faster than nature intended—sometimes need a little help remembering how to slow down and appreciate what we have, rather than constantly racing after what we desire.

Sloths are Nature's Zen masters of mellow. They have hung about the planet in one shape or another for more than 60 million years, outliving faster, flashier animals like the saber-toothed tiger. The secret to their success is their stealthy, sustainable slothful nature. So, take a leaf out of the sloths' serene book—it could benefit not just you, but the rest of planet Earth.

—Lucy Cooke

Slow and steady wins the race.

—Aesop

If you live in awareness,
it is easy to see
miracles everywhere.

—*Thich Nhat Hanh*

TAKE IT SLOW

Sloths may appear to be sluggish, but they're not inappropriately idle. It's both an adaptation to spend less energy and a defense mechanism against predators. Being motionless helps sloths blend in with the trees, and their slow movements slip under the radar of sharp-eyed foes like the fast-flying harpy eagle.

Happiness never decreases by being shared.

—Buddha

You need to let
little things that
would ordinarily
bore you suddenly
thrill you.

—*Andy Warhol*

Sleep's what we need.
It produces an emptiness
in us into which sooner
or later energies flow.

–*John Cage*

SAVOR THE SWEETER THINGS IN LIFE

Sloths subsist on a lean and green low-energy diet of leaves that provides them with just 160 calories a day. Their only indulgence is the occasional hibiscus flower—the equivalent of sloth chocolate—which they eat petal by petal.

For fast-acting relief,
try slowing down.

—*Jane Wagner*

Wait. Be patient.
The storm will pass.
The spring will come.

—*Robert H. Schuller*

There is no hurry.
We shall get there
some day.

—A. A. Milne

If you see someone without a smile, give 'em yours.

–Dolly Parton

LIVE IN THE MOMENT

Sloths are found only in the jungles of Central and South America—the land of the siesta and home of the hammock. Could this be a coincidence? Most sloths spend around 60 percent of their time resting—either asleep or in a waking, meditative state—so perhaps not.

It's the simple things in life that are the most extraordinary.

—Paulo Coelho

Happiness, knowledge, not in another place but this place, not for another hour, but this hour.

—*Walt Whitman*

Wherever you go, there you are.

—Jon Kabat-Zinn

DON'T SWEAT IT

Supercool three-toed sloths don't sweat—literally—because they have no sweat glands. Two-toed sloths have some sweat glands, on their snout, for example, but none are present on their feet, so there's no danger of them slipping from the trees.

Miraculous turns of fate can happen to those who persist in showing up.

—*Elizabeth Gilbert*

Don't worry about a thing.

—*Bob Marley*

If you smile when no one else is around, you really mean it.

—Andy Rooney

If your eyes are blinded with your worries, you cannot see the beauty of the sunset.

—*Jiddu Krishnamurti*

IT'S ALL ABOUT THE JOURNEY

One of the keys to sloth life is persistence—these travelers keep climbing in the superhighway of the treetops on a never-ending quest for tasty leaves and sunny spots. Their motto is "Don't hurry, be happy!" Sloths don't flinch nervously or react to noises, so they can truly chill out and enjoy the ride. And they can cover quite a bit of area: In the wild, sloths roam a range the size of five soccer fields.

Our life is frittered away by detail. . . . Simplify, simplify.

—Henry David Thoreau

Life is full
of delightful
treasures, if we
take a moment to
appreciate them.

—*Oprah Winfrey*

Be here now and savor the delight of the present moment.

—Deepak Chopra

Do not worry that your life
is turning upside down. How
do you know that the side
you are used to is better
than the one to come?

—*Rumi*

Have patience
with all things, but
chiefly have patience
with yourself.

—*St. Francis de Sales*

EMBRACE SOLITUDE

Sloths are naturally introverted creatures and are very content to be alone—they don't need to seek out company. Although they don't *mind* socialization, most of their time is spent by themselves, peacefully communing with nature in their slow-moving, arboreal journey.

Let everything happen
to you: beauty and terror.
Just keep going.

−*Rainer Maria Rilke*

Almost everything will work again if you unplug it for a few minutes, including you.

–*Anne Lamott*

ALWAYS WEAR A SMILE

From the moment they're born, sloths have a serene and content look on their face. With an upturned mouth that gives the appearance of a permanent smile and a benevolent gaze that seems to suggest wisdom beyond their years, sloths are the picture of joyful serenity.

Forever is composed of nows.

—*Emily Dickinson*

Every mountaintop
is within reach if you just
keep climbing.

—*Barry Finlay*

Turn your face
to the sun and the shadows
will fall behind you.

—*Proverb*

DON'T RUSH

Sloths don't hop from tree to tree in a blaze of glory—they gently test the next branch to see if it's sound before they proceed. They move with the stealth and control of a Tai Chi master and are physically incapable of going faster than 1 mile per hour, since their muscles are engineered to move 15 times slower than other mammals.

Because inner peace and inner joy are independent of worldly circumstances, they are available to you anyplace and anytime.

—Chade-Meng Tan

If you are in a hurry, walk slowly. If you are even more in a hurry, take a detour.

—*Japanese proverb*

If you want to conquer the anxiety of life, live in the moment, live in the breath.

–Amit Ray

PERSPECTIVE IS EVERYTHING

Sloths sleep, eat, and even give birth upside down. They are specially equipped to be in that peculiar position—their organs are anchored to their rib cage so it doesn't hurt to breathe while they're hanging out.

However, that's not the only thing that's unusual about their perspective. Most mammals have seven neck vertebrae, including giraffes. But three-toed sloths have evolved their top two ribs into extra neck bones, so they can turn their head 270 degrees (and keep smiling), even when they are upside down.

The invariable mark of wisdom is to see the miraculous in the common.

—*Ralph Waldo Emerson*

You don't have to move fast or far. You can just go an inch. You can mark your progress breath by breath.

—*Cheryl Strayed*

May we go to the places that scare us.

–Pema Chödrön

STAY COOL

The body temperature of a sloth is the lowest of all mammals. It changes in response to the environment, like a reptile's. Not only can sloths keep cool internally, but they also have been known to drop from their treetop perches and plunge into a body of water for a swim. Surprisingly, sloths are excellent swimmers—their long arms help them take efficient strokes.

I am a slow walker,
but I never walk back.

—Abraham Lincoln

For quiet, sensitive souls, solitude is the golden thread that unites us with our inner world.

—Michaela Chung

You never really understand
a person until you consider
things from his point of view.

—*Harper Lee*

TURN A NEGATIVE INTO A POSITIVE

Sloths are good at using everything that's available to them, even some biological side effects that might seem a bit unsavory . . . like trapped wind. The sloth's leafy diet produces a lot of excess gas, which the sloth uses as a built-in buoyancy device to help keep it afloat when swimming (something sloths are remarkably good at).

When you get into a tight place,
and everything goes against you
till it seems as if you couldn't hold on
a minute longer, *never give up
then*, for that's just the place and
time that the tide'll turn.

—*Harriet Beecher Stowe*

Surrender to what is.
Let go of what was. Have
faith in what will be.

—Sonia Ricotti

Adopt the pace of Nature.
Her secret is patience.

—*Ralph Waldo Emerson*

GREAT ACHIEVEMENTS TAKE TIME

Sloths are exceptional when it comes to digestion, capable of eating toxic leaves that would make other animals sick. Their secret weapon is a large stomach and a lot of time. It can take an entire month for sloths to digest a single leaf—if the process went faster, they would poison themselves.

You better slow down.

—*The Beatles*

A good laugh and a long sleep are the two best cures for anything.

—*Irish proverb*

Imperturbable, resolute,
tree-like, slow to speak—
such a one is near
to Goodness.

—*Confucius*

IT'S OKAY TO STAND OUT . . .

Sloths are a sentinel species. This means that on a macro level, their performance in the rainforest environment is indicative of the well-being of the entire ecosystem.

. . .AND IT'S OKAY TO BLEND IN

On a micro level, sloths are an ecosystem unto themselves: They host moths and other insect species that can be found nowhere else. And their fur is covered in algae, which provides protective camouflage.

Whoever is happy will make others happy too.

—Anne Frank

It is a mistake to look too far ahead. Only one link of the chain of destiny can be handled at a time.

—*Winston Churchill*

The universe is full of magical things patiently waiting for our wits to grow sharper.

—*Eden Phillpotts*

HUG IT OUT

Baby sloths are born to hug so they can hang on tight to mom high up in the trees for the first six to nine months of their lives. They'll cling to anything—branches, arms, even stuffed animals. Adults become the ultimate tree-huggers, embracing the natural rhythms of their forest home.

Some journeys in life can only be traveled alone.

—*Ken Poirot*

It's enough for me to
be sure that you and I exist
at this moment.

–Gabriel García Márquez

It is hard work and great art to make life not so serious.

–*John Irving*

UNIQUENESS IS AN ADVANTAGE

Sloths are unique in many ways. They have hooks for hands, which may seem awkward, but it's one of the secrets to a slow lifestyle. Hooks enable sloths to hang from a tree like a hairy hammock and expend very little energy. (They're also handy for scratching remote itches.)

We shall not cease from exploration
And the end of all our exploring
Will be to arrive where we started
And know the place for the first time.

—*T. S. Eliot*

You're only here for a short visit.
Don't hurry. Don't worry.
And be sure to smell the flowers
along the way.

—*Walter Hagen*

Life isn't as serious as [the] mind makes it out to be.

—*Eckhart Tolle*

SLEEP IS SACRED

Two-toed sloths are almost exclusively nocturnal. They sleep all day long, high up in the trees, and spend their nights eating under the cover of darkness. On the other hand, three-toed sloths don't care whether it's day or night—they nap and snack around the clock.

Wisely and slow; they stumble that run fast.

–*William Shakespeare*

Life has taught us that love does not consist in gazing at each other but in looking outward together in the same direction.

—*Antoine de Saint-Exupéry*

ACKNOWLEDGMENTS

First, I have to thank the sloths for being such inspirational creatures. But I also need to give a massive sloth hug to the extraordinary people and organizations that work so hard to understand and protect these exceptional creatures. You have taught me everything I know about sloths—I am in awe of you all. Becky Cliffe of the Sloth Conservation Foundation and Sam Trull of the Sloth Institute have both been especially generous with their incredible knowledge over the years. Leslie Howle, founder of the Toucan Rescue Ranch in Costa Rica, is a woman who rarely sleeps in order to save sloths (thanks also to her husband, Jorge; Pedro; and Carol, her right-hand woman at TRR). Thanks to Nestor Correa and Yiscel Yanguez of APPC (Asociación Panamericana para la Conservación) and the Gamboa Wildlife Center in Panama, and to the Jaguar Rescue Center and Kids Saving the Rainforest (both in Costa Rica) for allowing me into your world to photograph your rescued sloths. Finally, thanks to Nisha Owen and the EDGE of Existence program at the Zoological Society of London for your tireless work protecting the endangered pygmy and maned sloths.

To join the Sloth Appreciation Society and find out the very latest about the sloths' slow movement, visit slothville.com.

Sloth Conservation Foundation **slothconservation.com**
The Sloth Institute **theslothinstitutecostarica.org**
Toucan Rescue Ranch **toucanrescueranch.org**
Asociación Panamericana para la Conservación **appcpanama.org**
Jaguar Rescue Center Foundation **jaguarrescue.foundation**
Kids Saving the Rainforest **kidssavingtherainforest.org**
EDGE of Existence **edgeofexistence.org**
Zoological Society of London **zsl.org**